KNOW ABOUT

SMOKING

by Margaret O. Hyde

illustrated by Dennis Kendrick

Do you have a good answer for someone who insists that you smoke? Most young people say that they never want to begin smoking. Some try to stop parents and friends, but pick up the habit themselves in spite of their good intentions. The pressures to begin smoking can be resisted more easily if one sees through them.

Here are some suggestions to help you feel comfortable about refusing your first cigarette, along with information about the immediate and long-term hazards of smoking and how easily one can become addicted to nicotine. The history of smoking and the friction between smokers and nonsmokers are also explored.

Recent reports indicate that resisting the temptation to smoke is more important than was suspected in the past. This book will help you to KNOW ABOUT SMOKING and avoid the habit most smokers wish they could break.

For Emily Goodrich Hyde

KNOW ABOUT SMOKING

by
Margaret O. Hyde
Illustrated by Dennis Kendrick

McGraw-Hill Book Company

New York   St. Louis   San Francisco   Auckland   Bogotá
Hamburg   Johannesburg   London   Madrid   Mexico
New Delhi   Panama   Paris   São Paulo
Singapore   Sydney   Tokyo   Toronto

3 4 5 6 7 8 9 10 11   BKP BKP   8 9 8 7 6

ISBN 0-07-031671-6

LIBRARY OF CONGRESS CATALOGING IN PUBLICATION DATA
Hyde, Margaret Oldroyd, 1917-
    Know about smoking.

    Bibliography: p.
    1. Smoking. 2. Cigarette habit.   I. Title.
HV5733.H93   1982   362.2'9   82-14953
ISBN 0-07-031671-6

The author wishes to thank the many people who contributed ideas for this book. Dr. John K. Worden of the Vermont Lung Center was especially helpful.

CONTENTS

1.

Could This Happen to You?

"Smoke? Not me!"

That is what Ted said when he was twelve years old. He is a junior in college now and he smokes a pack of cigarettes every day. Ted has been trying to break his smoking habit for three years. Actually, one time he did stop for a month.

These days Ted often asks himself, "Why did I ever start to smoke when I was so sure that I never would?"

Twenty-year-old Marcia said she would never start smoking. That was long ago, before she went to junior high school. There she met some girls who laughed at her because she refused a cigarette, so she decided to try one.

She hated the taste of her first cigarette. What was even more unpleasant, the smoke irritated her throat and made her cough. To top it all off, she began to feel queasy after smoking part of the cigarette. Marcia had heard that no one likes smoking when they start, so she tried several cigarettes. Before long she began to enjoy smoking.

Now Marcia smokes at least a dozen cigarettes every day. She still doesn't like the way her mouth feels in the morning. She still feels guilty about polluting the air for her nonsmoking friends. And she finds her habit a nuisance when she's in a place where smoking is prohibited and she gets a strong desire to smoke. Sometimes she feels the same way she did in junior high school. People seem to be laughing at her. But now it is because she hasn't been able to stop smoking.

Susan is a teenage mother and a former champion tennis player. She never smoked before her baby was born. Then she found herself missing the companionship of her friends. With most of her time spent rushing around trying to keep up with the diaper changing, the washing, the shopping, the cleaning, and what seemed like an endless number of jobs that were never finished, Susan decided she owed herself a break and started smoking. Now when the baby is asleep, she curls up in her favorite chair, reads a good book, and enjoys her cigarette.

Susan finds herself smoking many other times during the day, however, even when she's not relaxing. She lights a cigarette when things are especially hectic, or just when she feels like smoking. Still, there are many times when Susan wishes she had never developed the habit. This is especially true when the baby is asleep in his crib and Susan discovers that there are no cigarettes in the house. She was so frustrated one evening that she stooped to smoking some long butts that had been left in the ashtray. She hated herself for needing a cigarette so badly; but, more than that, she was worried. Susan began to wonder whether smoking would cut down on her performance in tennis, for she hopes to resume playing competitively when her baby is a little older.

Tim is a good baby-sitter. He lives in an area where there are more sitters than children who need them, so he is glad that the neighborhood parents as well as their little kids like him. For a while, Tim had all the jobs he could handle. But then word of his smoking got around and his jobs dwindled. Several parents were frank about the matter. They told him they would call him again if they could be sure he had stopped smoking.

Most people under twelve are sure that they will never start to smoke. They are aware of the health hazards, especially for adults who have smoked for a long time. Trying to get parents to stop smoking is a common goal among children. Today's young people are fortunate that there is a changing attitude about smoking. Actually, most people in the United States do not smoke.

In 1980 the percentage of women who smoked dropped to the lowest level in fifteen years. According to the National Center for Health Statistics, the percentage of all Americans seventeen years and older who smoked was a whole percentage point lower than it had been the year before. In 1981 the director of the National Institute of Drug Abuse said that there had been a dramatic cutback in cigarette smoking by young people, although some youngsters—especially girls—were beginning to smoke at an earlier age than was common in the past. In 1982 the Institute reported the results of a survey which found that daily smoking among high-school seniors had dropped from 29 percent to 20 percent over a period of four years.

This anti-smoking trend is beginning to filter down to some of the people who have not yet started, making it easier for them to resist the pressures that are responsible for most people's early smoking habits.

Today's young people are fortunate in another

way, too. There are an increasing number of programs in elementary schools throughout the country that "inoculate" them against smoking.

2.

Inoculation Against Smoking

According to the American Cancer Society, at least 45 million of today's 54 million smokers wish they could stop. If this is the case, why do so many people start in the first place? Do they fear being different, as Marcia did? Do they think smoking will relax them, as Susan did? Do they hope that smoking will help them cover up their awkwardness and shyness? Do they worry that they will be called "chicken" if they don't smoke?

What can you say when someone accuses you of being afraid to smoke? There *are* some easy answers, whether you are being pushed to smoke tobacco or marijuana.

Molly learned a good answer through a skit that was part of a so-called inoculation program in her social-studies class. In the skit, Molly's friends Bill,

Mary, and Tim played the parts of teenagers who smoked. Molly's character was someone who had decided not to smoke and resisted being branded a weirdo when she refused a cigarette that was offered to her.

In the skit, Molly walked over to talk with Bill, Mary, and Tim, who were standing together with their backs toward her. Molly hadn't realized they were smoking until she joined them. Tim offered Molly a cigarette, but she turned it down.

"Come on, Molly," taunted Bill. "Don't be chicken. Join the group."

Molly refused to be baited. Instead, she laughed and said, "I would be more of a chicken if I smoked just to impress you." Then she smiled at Bill and quickly steered the conversation to another subject.

Molly and other people in her class who did not want to be pressured into smoking practiced this straightforward and simple refusal many times.

Sometimes they used a slightly different reply when someone called them chicken. "If I smoke to prove to you that I'm not chicken," they'd say, "all I'll really be doing is showing you that I'm afraid not to smoke when you want me to. I don't want to smoke."

Through this process known as inoculation,

many school programs are toughening up young people who don't want to start smoking. Much as people can be inoculated against germs, they can be protected from the social pressures that encourage them to smoke. Boys and girls who have not yet started smoking can be exposed to a weak dose of "social germs" and thus learn the necessary skills to resist stronger pressure from their peers.

The inoculation method demonstrated in the skit starring Molly and her friends is called role playing. Actually, role playing is used as a way to prepare people for many kinds of situations. Secret service men, FBI agents, sheriffs, detectives, and a wide variety of specialists who work with people are trained this way. In a totally nonthreatening environment, participants can rehearse skills which can then be used in more highly pressured situations when their emotions might interfere with their intentions. Role playing is a way of making certain that one can stay in control, and it is especially helpful for those who do not want to be talked into smoking.

Molly's class practiced role playing in a variety of skits. In one of them, her classmate John played the part of a boy who encounters some people he barely knows at a party. John isn't at the gathering long before he discovers that he is the only non-smoker. He wants to feel accepted, but he really doesn't want to start smoking.

Someone in the skit remarks, "Everyone smokes. Why don't you?"

John picks up a cigarette and looks at it. He considers the statistics he has read about how many people smoke and how many do not, and he pauses to think. He knows that smokers belong to a minority group and that their numbers are declining. John does not want to be different — he wears the same kind of clothes his classmates wear, listens to the same kind of music — and since most teenagers do not smoke, he feels he really isn't different if he doesn't smoke. Most of his old friends don't smoke. And if the people at the party really want to be his friends, they won't care whether or not he smokes.

John mentions to his new acquaintances the trouble that his brother is having trying to quit smoking. He puts the cigarette down without lighting it and remarks casually that he doesn't want to go through the agony of quitting.

The boy who offered the cigarette to John admits that for three months he has been trying to stop smoking. John smiles. He knows that most of the people who smoke wish they had never started.

John feels good about himself.

Sue practices dealing with an angry smoker in a skit that involves her waiting in line at the movies. Someone in front of her is blowing smoke in her face, and Sue makes a gesture that indicates her annoyance, but the smoker ignores it. Finally Sue speaks up and asks the person not to blow the smoke in her direction. The smoker gets angry and tells Sue to grow up. She practices some reasonable arguments she can use if she ever really finds herself in such a situation.

In another skit, health hazards are emphasized by having one person play the part of a doctor who has the unpleasant task of telling a man he must stop smoking because he has developed lung cancer. And in still another skit, a person who is struggling for breath because of a disease called emphysema begs the doctor to help him stop the smoking that contributed to his illness. He seems unable to quit on his own despite the discomfort and seriousness of the disease.

A very popular skit is one in which a son or daughter tries to persuade a parent to stop smoking. One of the arguments used by the young people points out that more than a hundred life-insurance companies offer special rates for non-smokers because their life expectancy is greater.

Children ask their parents why they knowingly engage in such self-destructive behavior when they direct so much of their energy toward preserving their lives.

In all these skits, actors exchange parts and repeat the action. Afterward, there are class discussions in which boys and girls are asked to anticipate situations where they will be able to resist peer pressure to smoke.

For example, imagine that you are hanging around the park after school when Jim, a new acquaintance, takes out a cigarette and lights up. You can expect to be bugged if you do not accept the cigarette he will probably offer you.

Now imagine what you will say to him. Maybe it will just be a simple "No," while you tell yourself you don't have to smoke a stinking cigarette just to show you're cool and that if Jim was really cool he would not have to smoke to show off. Consider that you can walk away to do an errand if the pressure on you becomes too great. And all the time you can be realizing how satisfying it feels to be so independent. Many young people are using this same technique to avoid becoming involved with marijuana smokers.

Role playing is just one part of anti-smoking inoculation. Another part involves examining the reasons why you do not want to begin smoking. Some of these may be: avoiding bad breath, reduced athletic stamina, stained teeth, and smelly clothing; not wanting to get hooked; and wanting control of your own actions and a sense of well-being.

In today's world smoking is no longer considered socially acceptable by the majority of people, so social problems might be included in a list of reasons for not starting to smoke. For example, people who smoke become self-conscious when they have to ask for an ashtray in another person's home. Finding a seat in the smoking section of a plane, train, or other area can be inconvenient.

After listing these and other reasons why persons do not want to smoke, students who are being inoculated are asked why they want to smoke. One of the most common reasons is pressure from friends. Feeling more grown-up is another reason young people give for smoking. However, using smoking as a rite of passage to the grown-up world is becoming less popular. Intelligent people no longer consider smoking a symbol of adulthood since most adults who smoke wish they had never started.

Another once-common reason for starting to smoke is also disappearing. At one time, young smokers were believed to be rejecting the authority of their parents. Study after study has shown, however, that parents who smoke are likely to have children who smoke. In fact, teenagers who have two parents who smoke are twice as likely to smoke as those with nonsmoking parents. Smoking by these young people can hardly be considered a form of adolescent rebellion.

One part of any program to inoculate people against starting to smoke often consists of asking a group to write down their ideas about what kinds of people smoke. In one study, about 68 percent of the teenagers thought that teachers were likely to be smokers. But an American Cancer Society survey found that only 23 percent of female teachers and 18 percent of male teachers actually smoke.

Much the same was true when groups of young people were asked to estimate how many of their own group smoked. The answers were much higher than the actual number who reported smoking even in tests in which smokers could not be identified.

"Everybody smokes," is a statement that is often made by smokers who want others to join them, but statistics show that it is farther from the truth than it ever has been. And as more and more young people inoculate themselves against developing the habit, and as more nonsmokers fight for their rights to breathe fresh air, the anti-smoking trend should continue to grow.

3.

What Most Smokers Don't Know

Bill is a thirty-five-year-old father whose friends are concerned about the large number of cigarettes he smokes each day. He says he knows about the health hazards but would rather smoke than live longer. Bill is tired of hearing nonsmokers complain about having to share the air that he pollutes. His latest answer to nonsmokers amuses him greatly. When someone complains about the smoke in the air, Bill suggests that the person think of him as a human filter.

"Cigarette smoke is a very complex material containing extremely tiny particles that are breathed in by the smoker so that they reach the farthest parts of the lung," Bill says. "Each time I smoke, I breathe in about a million particles for each cubic centimeter. Since only about 20 per-

cent of these particles are exhaled, 80 percent of them are retained in my lungs. So, you see, I am really a human filter."

This idea just reenforces the resolve of the non-smokers. They laugh at Bill. If they realized that the particles from just two cigarettes an hour accumulate to an amount greater than that considered safe by the Environmental Protection Agency, however, they might protest even harder to try to stop Bill from fouling the air they breathe.

Some smokers argue that there is too much talk these days about things that are bad for people. They say there is pollution in the air from buses and cars and wood and coal smoke, and that this kind of air pollution can be as much a cause of lung cancer as cigarette smoke. This is undeniably true. But what the smokers fail to realize is that their own smoking makes our admittedly polluted air even worse.

Most smokers are vaguely aware of the health hazards of smoking. Still, many indulge in a kind of magical thinking in which they are certain that the things that happen to other smokers will not happen to them. For example, more than half of the young people who smoke believe that the dangers of smoking are exaggerated for their age group. And many believe that all of the health hazards associated with smoking happen only to older people. These youngsters are unaware of the many short-term effects of smoking.

Almost everyone knows that dirt goes into the lungs along with the air one breathes. Particles are trapped by mucus, a sticky material that is secreted by glands in the walls of the air passage. Every healthy person's lungs contain short hairlike bristles known as cilia, which sweep up and out, pushing mucus, germs, and dirt away. Even one cigarette slows down the cilia that work to sweep out the dirt and germs, and heavy smoking destroys them completely.

If the cilia are not strong enough to sweep away the accumulation of "garbage" in the lungs, people cough or sneeze to blast the foreign material out. Perhaps you have noticed that people who smoke a lot also cough a lot—and some of them don't even know why.

Before there was some control over cigarette advertising, one company used the slogan, "Not a Cough in a Carload." Even in those days, some smokers must have been conscious of the fact that smoking made them cough.

Since cilia that have been damaged can no longer act like brooms to sweep germs, mucus, and dirt out of the lungs, it is not surprising to find

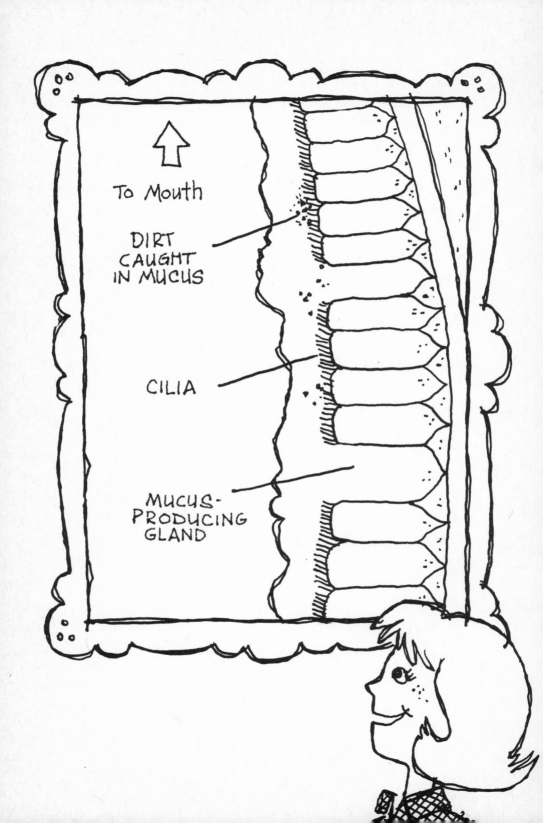

studies that estimate smokers are sick in bed 88 million more days each year than nonsmokers.

Of course, the longer you smoke the deadlier are the habit's effects. But it doesn't take years for smoking to hurt you. Students in one class project were taught by the school nurse to measure a person's vital signs, before and after he smoked just one cigarette. It was obvious to them from their research that this small amount of smoking sped up the heartbeat, increased blood pressure, decreased lung capacity, and caused a drop in the skin temperature of fingers and toes.

Many smokers say that cigarettes relax them. But these people don't know that nicotine's effect on the body resembles that of such stimulants as coffee and amphetamine (speed) rather than sedatives (downers). Certainly, cigarettes make people who are addicted to nicotine feel calmer, but that is only because the cigarettes prevent withdrawal symptoms.

Many smokers claim that nicotine is not like any other addicting substance because it doesn't interfere with normal behavior. New research indicates that quite the opposite is true. Heavy smokers need nicotine, and possibly other chemicals found in cigarette smoke, in order to avoid drowsiness and to focus their attention.

Some smokers know that tobacco smoke yellows teeth—especially if they are familiar with those radio and TV ads for a tooth polish made especially to clean away the stain on smokers' teeth. But many smokers do not realize how unpleasant their breath and their clothing smell. Nonsmokers who enter smokers' homes often notice that the odor has penetrated the furnishings. More than one person has wondered why women who smoke bother to buy expensive perfumes, since the fragrances are overshadowed by the aroma of tobacco smoke. But smokers tend to be oblivious to the smelly side effects of their habit because continued smoking often diminishes their sense of smell—and their sense of taste, for that matter.

Many smokers who see No Smoking signs in their dentists' offices think that the signs have been placed there for the dentists' comfort. These people don't realize that smoking delays the healing of mouth sores and contributes to gum disease, a condition that often leads to tooth loss.

Carbon monoxide is seldom blamed for damage to a smoker's health, even though it has an adverse effect on people of all ages. This gas is now known to be one of the most harmful ingredients in cigarette smoke. It literally drives the oxygen out of the red blood cells. The level of carbon monoxide in a smoker's blood is four times higher than normal, and it can be as much as fifteen times higher in the blood of heavy smokers. Carbon monoxide stays in a person's bloodstream as long as six hours after he or she stops smoking, reducing the amount of oxygen delivered to the many cells of the body.

There is evidence that the levels of carbon monoxide found in cigarette smoke decrease physical performance. Athletes have been discouraged from smoking for years, but the reasons for this were not always known. Low levels of carbon monoxide may also have a slightly negative effect on attentiveness and the ability to think.

While carbon monoxide is harmful to everyone, it is especially damaging to people with heart or lung disease. And a pregnant woman who smokes two packs of cigarettes a day blocks off 40 percent of the oxygen to her unborn child. Carbon monoxide is thought to be the most important factor in causing spontaneous abortion, stillbirth, and reduced birth weight in babies.

Women who smoke and take birth-control pills are many times as likely to suffer heart attacks and strokes as women who do neither.

Smoking hazards for future parents are better known for women than for men. However, recent

studies indicate that men who smoke tobacco are more likely than nonsmokers to produce abnormal sperm, and this can lead to infertility or cause birth defects.

The health hazards associated with smoking are grim indeed, and perhaps you feel you've read enough about them. But if you really want to know more facts for yourself or to help convince a parent or friend to stop smoking, consider these statements which are based on numerous research studies:

The earlier one starts to smoke, the more likely one is to die from smoking-related diseases.

Each year, six times as many people in the United States die from smoking-related causes as die from automobile accidents.

Smoking contributes to at least 80 percent of all deaths from lung cancer.

Smoking nearly doubles a person's risk of heart attack. Cigarette smoking is believed to account for one-third of all deaths from heart disease.

Cigarette smoke has about two-thousand other things in it in addition to "tar," nicotine, and carbon monoxide. Although less is known about these substances, many of them are considered harmful and some are known to cause cancer in certain animals.

Cigarette smoking has been established as a significant cause of cancer of the larynx, oral cavity, esophagus, and bladder, and it has been associated with other cancers, too.

These are just some of the ways in which smoking affects health. Still, a large number of people do not believe that they will personally suffer the health consequences of smoking. One-third of the people polled in a number of studies were unaware that most cases of emphysema, a disease in which people have difficulty breathing, were caused by smoking. More than 40 percent did not know that studies indicate that smoking causes most cases of lung cancer. The list of what smokers do not know is long.

Smokers may know that there is a warning on every advertisement for cigarettes and on each package, but a recent study by the Federal Trade Commission showed that most people do not really notice the warning. Only about 3 percent of the adults questioned actually read the warning.

Suggestions for new warnings include the following:

LUNG CANCER: The major cause is smoking.

HEART ATTACK: A major risk factor for smokers.

TEENS: The earlier you start to smoke, the

more likely you are to die from smoking.

The most important message is obvious: DON'T START TO SMOKE!

4.

Smokers vs. Nonsmokers for Hundreds of Years

The battle between smokers and nonsmokers has been waging for hundreds of years. Columbus and other explorers who came to America from the Old World reported seeing Indians "setting fire to rolls of dried leaves." Sailors on the early ships tried "drinking the smoke" that came from the "fire," and they, too, found pleasure in this custom. They also found that after they had smoked for a few days, they had to continue to do so to avoid the discomfort that only more smoking could relieve.

As long ago as the sixteenth century, Portuguese sailors brought tobacco to the many trading posts on their sea routes. They carried the seeds with them and started small tobacco farms wherever they voyaged. In this way they were able to meet their own needs as well as to supply tobacco for gifts and bartering.

These tobacco farms were soon under the control of the local inhabitants. Natives of such far-away places as Polynesia and the Philippines learned to smoke, and the tobacco habit spread to parts of Europe, the Americas, Asia, Africa, and Australia.

The "rights of nonsmokers" is a rather new expression, but nonsmokers have been complaining about smoking for hundreds of years. People who smoked have long been described as indulging in a disgusting habit which they find impossible to give up. During periods of history when the price of tobacco rose because the plant was scarce, some smokers were accused of spending money for tobacco when they had no money left for food.

One famous quote that dates back to 1610 suggests that the estate of a nobleman who smokes "runs out through his nose."

Early arguments against smokers were often more heated than they are today, and some reactions against smoking have been severe, indeed. In the seventeenth century, Pope Urban VIII issued a formal bill against tobacco, sealed with the Fisherman's ring in 1642, and Pope Innocent X issued another in 1650. At about the same time in

Russia, castration was a possible sentence for repeated offenders.

Health hazards were not considered a major argument against smoking in past centuries because early smokers were unaware of the risks involved. But smoking-related fires then were even more of a problem than they are now. Since buildings were more combustible, whole sections of a city could be destroyed by a single blaze started by a careless smoker. Distrust of the alien origin of tobacco was another reason for anti-smoking sentiments.

Despite these objections — and the fact that cigarettes with paper wrappers were not manufactured until the eighteenth century — the habit of smoking spread quickly.

As early as 1575, Mexican priests were instructed by their council to forbid smoking in church. The Indians had been accustomed to smoking in their old places of worship, and they wanted to do the same during services in the Catholic church. Even the missionary priests who acquired the habit had to be restricted from smoking during religious services.

Snuff is powdered tobacco that is inhaled. Since it could be inconspicuously sniffed in church, some people used it as a substitute for smoking and as a source of the nicotine to which their bodies had become accustomed. Inhaling snuff was a popular custom in some countries for a period of time, but most people still preferred to smoke.

Law after law proved useless in stopping people from smoking. The habit spread among men in countries far and wide. Complaints about smokers continued, too, and some of the people who were opposed to smoking went to great extremes to try to stop the habit they hated.

In 1604, King James I of England expressed his opinion against smoking in a lengthy statement which concluded with these words: "A custom loathsome to the eye, hateful to the nose, harmful to the brain, dangerous to the lungs, and in the black stinking fume thereof, nearest resembling the horrible Stygian smoke of a pit that is bottomless."

But even after King James increased tobacco import taxes, smoking continued to spread throughout Great Britain.

In eighteenth-century Switzerland, heavy taxes on smoking were so unpopular that their removal may have been brought about by the fear of a revolution. There actually was a revolt in Berlin in 1848 that is believed to have been due partly to a ban on smoking in the streets.

Sultan Murad IV of Turkey is reported to have

decreed the death penalty for smoking in 1633 and to have ordered the execution of as many as eighteen people a day for smoking. This cruel sultan would surprise men who were smoking on the battlefield and punish the offenders by beheading or hanging them or by crushing their hands and feet. But even the fear of torture or death did not stop some of his soldiers from smoking.

The modern cigarette was introduced in the year 1913 by the Reynolds Tobacco Company under the name of Camels. This was the first time that different kinds of domestic tobacco were blended with highly aromatic Turkish tobaccos and sweeteners.

During the next sixty-five years the number of cigarettes that were smoked in America rose from about 18 billion a year to about 600 billion, and the skirmish over smokers' rights grew as the health hazards associated with cigarettes became more obvious.

5.

Smokers vs. Nonsmokers Today

Almost everyone knows someone who just cannot stop smoking, so it is not surprising to find that the habit of smoking has never been completely erased from a country in which people learned to use tobacco. However, the number of people who will give up cigarettes this year in the United States alone will probably be about a million. This is the number of people who have been stopping each year in the recent past, and the trend is increasing. The American Lung Association estimates that there are now almost 50 million Americans who are ex-smokers.

In some cases, people struggle to stop smoking in order to please other family members who seem more concerned about their health than the smokers themselves. Mothers of young children who are aware of the damage that can be done by "passive smoking" are included in this group.

Babies of parents who smoke are much more likely to contract pneumonia and other diseases involving the lungs than are children whose parents do not smoke. Slight differences in physical growth, behavior, and intelligence have been found in some children as old as eleven years.

Secondhand smoke is blamed for much illness, but not everyone agrees on the seriousness of this problem. In one study, children exposed to smoke in a small room for thirty minutes showed an increase in heart rate and blood pressure as well as a rise in the level of carbon monoxide in their blood. This gas replaces some of the oxygen that our bodies require.

Many people who do not smoke are expressing their concern about secondhand smoke in very noticeable ways. You may see buttons that read SMOKERS STINK and notice signs proclaiming that it is illegal to smoke in elevators and other public areas in some buildings. Trains, buses, and airplanes have special sections to segregate smokers and nonsmokers. Your doctor probably displays a No Smoking sign in his or her office.

The American Lung Association has found that

smoke from the end of a burning cigarette contains more harmful substances than the smoke that is actually inhaled by the smoker. This fact is of special concern to nonsmokers in a roomful of smokers.

Some nonsmokers who are fighting for their rights to breathe air that is not polluted with smoke have joined together in groups to press for laws prohibiting smoking in public places. One group is called S.H.A.M.E., which stands for the Society to Humiliate, Aggravate, Mortify, and Embarrass Smokers.

A taxi driver might display a sign in his cab reading YOUR RIGHT TO SMOKE ENDS WHERE MY NOSE BEGINS, but many people who object to smoking find themselves in situations where they cannot use signs to ask smokers to refrain from lighting up. Many of these people have caused hard feelings by demanding that smokers put out their cigarettes in restaurants or other public places, but there is a more pleasant way of getting results.

Suppose a man is puffing on his cigar at a restaurant table near a person who objects to his smoke. The nonsmoker gets up from her table, goes over to the cigar smoker, and says, "Sir, we have a problem."

"What do you mean?" asks the man, puffing away.

"You must smoke your cigar in order to enjoy your dinner, but I must be free of cigar smoke in order to enjoy mine."

The man laughs and puts out his cigar.

Not everyone will be as accommodating as this man, but many people will cooperate if approached in a gracious manner. Nonsmokers find that they can accomplish more by keeping calm and considering the smoker's point of view than by acting aggressively.

Many nonsmokers have learned to consider the fact that those who smoke often have no idea what people are talking about when they complain about the smell of smoke. Many smokers are unaware that their habit plays havoc with their own sense of smell.

Several years ago, groups who were trying to protect the rights of nonsmokers talked about the two-thirds of the population that does not smoke. Today, groups of nonsmokers aim to protect a larger percentage of the population—the three-fourths of the population who are not smokers.

6.

How Well Can You Read The Ads?

How can one sell a product when almost everyone agrees that it is harmful? Suppose it interferes with a person's sense of smell and taste and makes the user smell awful. The product is habit-forming, even addicting? It is expensive, shortens life span, and has countless negative side effects. The difficulties involved in getting people to buy it seem obvious, and yet the product, which you can recognize as cigarettes, sells very well.

Most of today's smokers are adults who began their smoking before they knew about the health hazards. Even though some two-thirds of these smokers would like to stop, only about one smoker in five succeeds in quitting permanently. According to one estimate, two-thirds of the people who ever started smoking still do so on a regular basis. This makes a good solid market for cigarette sales.

As mentioned earlier, the trend among young people is toward fewer smokers. Even though the tobacco industry advertises that smoking should be an adult custom and the decision to smoke should be made only by adults, they spend a great deal of money trying to persuade people to try smoking and to start smoking certain brands. And many young people get the message. Cigarettes are the most heavily advertised product in America. Almost half of the billboards in the United States advertise cigarettes. You are probably well aware of the large numbers of ads in newspapers and magazines. And if you use public transportation that carries advertising, you've been exposed to countless cigarette ads.

There are no cigarette ads on television and radio, however. In 1967 the Federal Trade Commission ruled that the "Fairness Doctrine" that had been applied to political campaigns should also apply to cigarette advertising. (This meant that advertisers had to give equal time to warnings on the risks of smoking.) The following year the Surgeon General appointed a task force to report on smoking and health. This task force reported that the industry was "encouraging death and disease." In 1971 the United States became the twelfth country to ban cigarette advertising from radio and television.

No one is sure exactly how much this law hurt the tobacco industry. There are reports that the tobacco industry itself pushed for the end to its own television time because the impact of anti-smoking messages was so great. How effectively could an ad encourage people to smoke when it was preceded by an announcement warning them that smoking was the number-one cause of preventable illness and death?

One form of promoting smoking that has replaced television and radio advertising is the sponsoring of music and sporting events by cigarette companies. This brings the companies' names—along with a pleasant kind of association—to the attention of large numbers of people.

Another recent kind of cigarette promotion is the use of discount coupons and free samples. One company has been giving away free cartons of cigarettes. Apparently, they expect to more than make back the cost of this give-away by converting the people who receive the samples to the habit of smoking that brand.

Today, as much as a billion dollars is spent each year by the companies who want you to smoke.

What are they saying? How well can you read their ads?

Consider the so-called low-tar cigarettes. There has been a rise in the amount of money being spent to advertise a bewildering number of new kinds of cigarettes that contain relatively low levels of tar and nicotine. *Tar* is the term given to the tiny particles in cigarette smoke that remain after the nicotine and water are removed by a filter—the solid matter of the tobacco blend that is transformed into vapor as it is smoked.

Tars are composed of thousands of different chemicals, some 30 percent of which appear to be involved in causing cancer. The Vermont Lung Association has observed that tar in cigarettes is the same as tar on the road. Since there is much evidence to show that the lower the tar content, the less harmful the cigarette, manufacturers have been engaging in what has been called a tar war. This is quite evident when one reads the ads.

Even a quick look at some cigarette ads soon makes it clear that the tar factor is an important selling point. The contest is quite evident when one ad asks the reader to quickly name the brand of cigarette that is lowest in tar. It points out that the winner last year was a different brand. The ad even gives you a hint that the brand you probably

think is lowest in tar content really isn't. In another advertisement, the company explains that the government reports on tar content are old. Now, their brand is lower.

Keeping up to date on the tar content of about two-hundred brands is difficult. Government workers buy two packs of each type in fifty different geographic locations, and about a hundred cigarettes of each brand are analyzed. By the time the government report is issued, the manufacturer may have changed the content of the cigarettes. This explains why some claims seem contradictory.

A report issued in 1981 by the Surgeon General of the United States was titled "The Changing Cigarette: The Health Consequences of Smoking." In this report, it was noted that the method used to test cigarettes by machine may not be accurate when compared with the way people actually smoke the cigarettes. Although the machines are meant to represent the average smoker, they may not puff as deeply or frequently as their human counterparts.

Many people gain a false sense of security when they switch to low-tar cigarettes, but often these people are actually inhaling more deeply and smoking more often because low-tar cigarettes are usually low in nicotine, too. To get enough of the nicotine they crave, the smokers take more and bigger puffs. Few of these people realize that they take in more tar and more carbon monoxide per unit of nicotine when they smoke the low-tar brands.

One critic has suggested that the industry is selling more cigarettes by taking advantage of the health worries of smokers. A person may have to smoke forty low-tar cigarettes instead of twenty regular ones to get his or her ration of nicotine.

The Harvard Medical School Health Letter suggests that there is good reason to believe that the new, milder cigarettes may hook more people on smoking than the "full-flavor" high-tar cigarettes. They are less harsh for the person who has never smoked, and thus increase the chances of continued smoking. This report, along with many others, also questions the value of low-tar cigarettes.

An ad of Great Britain's Health Education Council suggests that switching from a high-tar to a low-tar cigarette is like jumping from the thirty-sixth floor of a building instead of the thirty-ninth floor. Obviously, the low-tar cigarettes should not be considered safe. The only safe cigarette is no cigarette.

As far as the cigarette companies are concerned, a problem with lowering the tar in cigarettes is that it changes the flavor. One cigarette company advertises, "Give up double-digit tar without giving up flavor." Another claims to be the overwhelming flavor winner in the most rigorous research that has ever been completed. And still another boasts that smokers report a taste bonus from its brand.

What actually determines a cigarette's flavor? Today's cigarette manufacturers claim to have 1,400 different ingredients from which to choose, but they are very secretive about the combinations of flavorings they use.

Many people who worry about the hazards of smoking are afraid that these flavorings, whatever they are, might be just as harmful as the nicotine and tars that were removed. The most common flavorings appear to be cocoa, licorice, and fruit juices. That sounds harmless enough, but many flavorings combine with other chemicals and become harmful when they are burned with tobacco. Several years ago the National Cancer Institute reported that condensed tar from cocoa-flavored cigarettes caused more tumors in mice than those that had no cocoa. Health experts in the United States suggested that cocoa should not be added

to the tobacco used for cigarettes. In Great Britain this flavoring is not allowed in cigarettes. The ban will be lifted if manufacturers can produce studies that show it is not related to the growth of tumors.

Coumarin is another flavoring that has been widely used in the manufacture of cigarettes. It is found in a weed known as deertongue and blended with tobacco to improve the odor and taste of some cigarettes. When burned, it has been likened to the pleasant aroma of vanilla and newly mown hay. But coumarin has been shown to be a poison that damages the liver and other organs and acts as a cancer-producing agent in laboratory animals. Some cigarette manufacturers now use substitutes for coumarin and claim that they buy deertongue only for use in cigarettes sold outside the United States.

Since cigarette companies are free to add anything they wish to flavor their product, no one really knows what is being used. Each brand of cigarette has its own blend of substances, and there is reason to believe that many of these flavorings may be nullifying the benefits of decreased amounts of tar. Although groups that are concerned with the health hazards of smoking are conducting much research on the amounts and kinds of flavorings being used, cigarette ads that

boast of better taste reveal no pertinent information on the subject. Even if the government
insisted that flavorings be mentioned along with
the health-risk warning, many people would not
read that part of the ad.

Publicity concerning the health hazards of cigarettes may be of less concern to the tobacco
industry than the notion that it is no longer socially
acceptable to smoke in public. This negative image
of smoking is directly opposed to the one the ads
try to present. These ads feature healthy-looking,
sexually attractive models, who are usually
engaged in some high-status activity that most
people cannot afford. The implication is that if you
smoke the right brand, in some magical way you
will become as healthy and wealthy as the models.

In contrast, real smokers often look tired and
anything but "springtime fresh." They are cough-
ing instead of smiling. Some have lungs that are in
such bad shape that they wouldn't dream of
participating in the active sports shown in the ads.

Many young people are not fooled by ads de-
signed to appeal to such special groups as women
and "macho" males. They know that the girl who
has come a long way and smokes a slim cigarette is
not really liberated just because she's hooked on a
certain cigarette. And the man who smokes will

not become successful just because he smokes a "man's cigarette." Many young people identify the special land described in the ads picturing rugged mountains and streams as Cancer Country.

The fact that some people are immune to these massive appeals through advertising is indicated by one marketing report that classifies cigarette tobacco as a slow growth industry. There is a trend away from cigarette smoking in spite of an increase in population.

The peer pressure that once led many young people to begin smoking is working in reverse today. Models in fashion magazines no longer hold cigarettes in their hands. Many outstanding athletes, actors, actresses, musicians, and other famous people have chosen not to smoke. In some cases, they never started smoking; in others, they stopped for health reasons. This is especially true of physicians, many of whom have given up smoking due to pressure from their peers.

Many young people choose not to smoke because they do not want to be slaves to cigarettes. They want to be free. Being smoke-free is easiest for those who never start smoking. The choice is yours.

7.

Help For Smokers Who Want To Become Smoke-Free

Since most of the people who smoke admit that they would like to give up their habit, it is not surprising to find many books, articles, and programs intended to help them. Once a year, smokers all over the United States join in an effort not to smoke for at least one day when they take part in the Great American Smokeout. As many as 20 million people join the day-long effort. Some throw their cigarettes into bonfires, undergo hypnosis, eat carrot sticks provided by college students in rabbit suits, and enjoy the support of cheerleaders who urge them on throughout the day. Still, only a small percentage of all those wanting to break the habit will really succeed through this gimmick.

The American Cancer Society has a number of suggestions for smokers who want to quit:

1. Make a list of all the good things you get from smoking, such as something to do with your hands, a way to relax, a reward for hard work, or whatever benefits you think it brings. Then list all the bad things you get from smoking, such as foul breath, smoke-filled hair, yellowed fingers, health problems. Then, think about it all.

2. Make your habit as inconvenient as possible. For example: limit the places in which you will smoke—to the outdoors, perhaps; never smoke unless you are standing; lock your cigarettes in a hard-to-get-to place.

3. Decide to quit smoking one month from now on a certain day. Prepare for this day by starting to cut down, changing to a lower-tar brand, smoking less of each cigarette, and trying to relax more through increased use of exercise, deep breathing, or any other method that appeals to you. Replace a cigarette with a carrot or sugarless gum. On Q day, reward yourself with a manicure to give your hands a new look.

4. The American Cancer Society and a number of other organizations offer clinics in which you can share your experiences with others who are trying to break the smoking habit. These programs are

conducted by trained leaders who understand how to help smokers become nonsmokers.

Below are some additional tips that should be of help if you've decided to quit smoking.

Many people who have succeeded in breaking the cigarette habit encourage others by assuring them that the first few days are the hardest. They suggest breathing deeply every time you crave a cigarette. Two or three deep-breathing sessions each day can help a lot.

Keep all cigarettes and ashtrays out of sight. Remove or avoid things that act as clues for smoking a cigarette.

Drink extra glasses of water.

Increase your exercise regimen. Starting a new athletic program can be extremely helpful, especially if it is outdoors.

Try snacking on carrots, celery, or other low-calorie foods when you get the urge for a cigarette.

Twiddle a pencil to replace the cigarette that you are in the habit of holding between your fingers. Your body is programmed to the actions that go along with smoking. Finding a substitute for these can help.

Is smoking an addiction? Not everyone thinks so, and much depends on how one defines addiction. What does seem certain is that for some people the withdrawal from smoking appears to be similar to that from other drugs. Many people suffer from all or a number of the following symptoms when they first stop: dry mouth, indigestion, headache, hunger, constipation, giddiness, and bad temper.

Doctors report that nicotine from an inhaled cigarette reaches the brain in seven seconds, twice as fast as that from an intravenous injection in the arm. Thus, at the rate of ten puffs per cigarette, the pack-a-day smoker gets more than seventy-thousand "shots" of nicotine in a year. This is frequency unmatched by any other form of drug-taking. Some experts attribute the difficulty in giving up smoking to the fact that the unpleasant and dangerous effects of the habit develop very slowly while the pleasant ones are so immediate.

If one is addicted to nicotine, continued smoking may be an escape route from the unpleasant symptoms of withdrawal. When the level of nicotine in the body drops, another cigarette provides the nicotine one craves.

No matter what the reason, most people have difficulty giving up smoking once they have developed the habit. The longer the habit has been established, the harder it is for most people to stop. However, anyone who wants to break the habit

badly enough can do so. And practically everyone who has suffered the problems that plague smokers wishes they had made a decision not to start.

Many organizations offer literature, courses, or kits to help those who want to stop smoking. Some of these are:

American Cancer Society, Inc.
777 Third Avenue
New York, New York 10017

American Heart Association
7320 Greenville Avenue
Dallas, Texas 75231

American Lung Association
1740 Broadway
New York, New York 10019

The Five-Day Plan to Stop Smoking
6840 Eastern Avenue, N.W.
Washington, D.C. 20012

Narcotics Education, Inc.
6830 Laurel Street, N.W.
Washington, D.C. 20012

Office on Smoking and Health
Rockville, Maryland 20857

Smoking Bibliographies
Office of Cancer Communications
National Cancer Institute
Building 31
9000 Rockville Pike
Bethesda, Maryland 20205

Suggestions for Further Reading

Casewit, Curtis W. *The Stop Smoking Book For Teens.* New York: Messner, 1980.

Halper, Marilyn S. *How To Stop Smoking.* New York: Holt, Rinehart and Winston, 1980.

Hyde, Margaret O. *Addictions: Gambling, Smoking, Cocaine Use And Others.* New York: McGraw-Hill, 1978.

Hyde, Margaret O. *Know About Alcohol.* New York: McGraw-Hill, 1979.

Hyde, Margaret O. and Bruce G. Hyde. *Know About Drugs,* 2nd ed. New York: McGraw-Hill, 1979.

Matchan, Don C. *We Mind If You Smoke.* New York: Jove, 1977.

Report of the Surgeon General, *The Changing Cigarette: The Health Consequences Of Smoking.* Washington, D.C.: United States Public Health Service, Department of Health and Human Services, 1981.

Winter, Ruth. *The Scientific Case Against Smoking.* New York: Crown, 1980.

Index

ABOUT THE AUTHOR

Margaret O. Hyde is the author of many successful science books, including ADDICTIONS: Gambling, Smoking, Cocaine Use and Others; FEARS AND PHOBIAS; BRAIN-WASHING AND OTHER FORMS OF MIND CONTROL; and SPEAK OUT ON RAPE! in addition to KNOW ABOUT DRUGS, now in its Second Edition, and KNOW ABOUT ALCOHOL. Mrs. Hyde received her masters degree from Columbia University and an honorary doctor of letters degree from Beaver College, her alma mater. She and her husband reside in Burlington, Vermont.

ABOUT THE ARTIST

Illustrator **Dennis Kendrick** received his training in commercial art at the Paier School of Art in New Haven, Connecticut, where he is now a lecturer in graphic communications, in addition to freelancing as a graphic designer and illustrator, Mr. Kendrick has illustrated a number of children's books, including Seymour Simon's ABOUT THE FOODS YOU EAT, ABOUT YOUR BRAIN, and SILLY ANIMAL JOKES AND RIDDLES.

McGraw-Hill Book Company
1221 Avenue of the Americas
New York, N.Y. 10020